The Great Expansion

The Great Expansion

Prose and Poetry

Timothy Michael Earwood

Writers Club Press
San Jose New York Lincoln Shanghai

The Great Expansion
Prose and Poetry

Writers Club Press
an imprint of iUniverse.com, Inc.

For information address:
iUniverse.com, Inc.
5220 S 16th, Ste. 200
Lincoln, NE 68512
www.iuniverse.com

ISBN: 0-595-19501-6

Printed in the United States of America

Contents

The Great Expansion

Ode to Poetry

What is Poetry?

Is it in books? In libraries?

In people's heads and hearts?

Good poet. Bad. How can this be?

A poet is a poet, as a poem is a poem.

The worst poems are written well; the best, written poor.

Writing is a conformed art; poetry has no bounds.

Writing destroys poetry.

If a poet is not an artist, then he is just a writer.

See, poetry should be defined as the beauty of thought. The uniqueness.

Why must we use rules when what we want to say is defined outside the boundaries.

we push it.

Shove it.

Make it fit.

It won't, so we change a word. A line. A paragraph.

Ah, you say.

Little do you know that you're laughing at yourself.

Expountion

Blah, blah, blah! If you asked me to define life in three words, then that is what I would say. Now, if you asked me to expound, then I would tell you about the joy and luxury of cheap thrills, and meaningless conversations that fill every day to the point of exhaustive reality that makes you forget about wealth, image, consciousness, work, religion, politics, and everything else that we think means something, but is just a temporary escape from the illusion (that's what they say) of permanence;

The fact that after death there is nothing, and from the clocks chime to the cocks crow is but an instant and, but, for, etc...One measures a mile to be a universe and a second to a lifetime, but when it's gone, you'll never know that it was already past. I love you and you love me and life is irony in it's self. Who said that? Me! It was always me.

Something

New ways. Joy. Happiness. These are the things to live for. The new found joy that one feels when discovering something that seems special to only me. Me. Me. That is only what matters. As I sit here I think of nothing except the thought itself.

What will come of my life? Will I discover new things? Or will I slowly rot away? I can't help from thinking that one day I will find it. IT. You know it. The thing that makes me happy. Money? Oh, yes. Money will make things alright. If only for a little while. It will. I know that people say that money isn't everything. Money doesn't buy happiness. But, I wonder if they know what they are talking about. They. THEY. I really don't like THEY anyway.

There are always people who really do not know what they are talking about. Maybe it is a common conspiracy of idiots that are bound together in some kind of loose-knit club unknowing to them all.

You'll Never Know Me

The wind grew strong, the trees began to sway.

We bundled up, didn't know another way.

I looked across the room, the candlelight shone on your face.

The hint of sadness, as you stared off into space.

Lies, dishonest, it's engraved upon your stone.

I sit beside you, but I couldn't be more alone.

You hide behind misfortune, from truth you run away.

It's time to go now, there's nothing left to say.

I guess you'll never know 'cause you never took the time to show me.

And because it didn't show, you'll never get the chance to know me.

March

Bacchanal *Part I*

Seem may incere

Quiet, Can't you see the wee one,

Lurking behind the shadowed dark?

See, hear, taste, smell, touch anything,

And I say I know.

Cause these voices and experiment Bacchanal.

Grady, Grati, Grari *Part II*

Grady, Grati, Grari.

O Latin some of god.

List presence over precedent,

And wisdom over wit;

Wait wanderers, haste wonderers;

Grace those who don't quite fit.

Truedom *Part III*

Flowers that bloom in season are as expected as April rain.

But width of mass in volume are considered quite insane.

To think of a thought or ponder a pond;

To meditate; to concentrate,

Are all mad as mad in itself, as if belief of
anything is any right.

Skipping

la da di

who are we

us to be

pay a fee

wake

sleep

pay

pay

pay

die

The Blues

I want to live in a neighborhood...

where people do not honk their horns at 6:00 in the morning. People just have no respect for other people.

where people do not stomp on my ceiling (their floor) at 3:00 in the morning.

where airplanes do not drowned out every piece of audio equipment in the house.

where merchants do not round up to the nearest dollar to make a little extra.

where IF I was late paying rent by even one minute, my belongings would not be out front in big blue bags.

Irony of Life

Desperately searching through a window of paradise

unknown to me and any other soul looking for refuge.

I die time and time again the shallow death that can only speak in place of ignorance.

Why do we tale to the imagination of lies and liars when we know what we seek can never be found?

Death gawks in the image of beatitude only for fools who go looking in the bottom of wishing-wells

filled with coins and tokens of dreams and foolish attempts to beat out the loneliness from our souls.

Grating hopes into splinters of desolate dreams—

dreaming bewildered mad, mad reality for reality is nothing, so is nothing reality?

Is reality reality?

Or do we sense that our own existence is built upon others wishes?

Why do we cry, yell, laugh and fuck,

'til the day we die through chances of luck?

Must we wait to find essence that feeds on our bones,

after witches cackle since long set the tone

of our ignorance, die laughing of the irony of life?

KRC

Searching in Darkness, wondering when the sun went down.
Your thoughts are clouded, perception is hazy.
The field is an ocean, the floors are skies.
Depths pass through each other, outside becomes in.
Everything becomes simple, but complications wait in the end.
Nothingless. Nowness.

Dusk, Facing West

People are so alive when they pass me. The smile.
The laugh. At that moment in time, they are content.
Taking pictures.
The beautiful stars shine on all who adore them.
Never will they be in this realm again.

Our seconds pass by unnoticed until it's too late.
You can never relive anything.
Perhaps that is why we strive to stay young.
The only thing we had was a false sense of freedom.
Freedom, like now, could be recalled at anytime death decides
to intervene.

Afterlife

Graveyard robber. Cheating the system.
Don't look too hard, if you do you might miss them.
Afraid? You better be. You know why?
In the end you'll get yours for living a lie.

a lone vision

look across the plains as far as can see
clouds roll in & out
never mind the annoying cries
or the dour faces
bad mothers
why?
in a world that judges only by circumstance
justice runs away without a fleeting glance
never looking back
mockery is everywhere

Seize the Day

Will I ever find peace? Happiness? I know it's there. Dangling like a bone in front of a hungry dog that's waiting for it.

Why must I plan to mourn instead of joyously celebrating life?

Why must lament always be ahead of laughter, overflowing-joyous-happiness-excited laughter?

Are we dead already?

I did it again. I include everyone else into my mournful parade to my grave.

Another reason. Or not. I only hope there will be a parade instead of a procession.

I want to be happy! Live life to the fullest. I want to do everyone and everything. I want to be uncontainable.

Should it matter that people say that I'm insane if I'm truly happy? Do I have a responsibility to be sane? Not as long as I don't hurt anybody.

I WANT MY E-MAIL NOW!

Game of Life

The Weak are just our opponent's easy kill, as a pawn in a chess game, they are worthless and easy taking, but at the same time, deadly when needed.

In a world that chuckles O so amazingly at those who can only stand on the thread of hope that society offers them as a token to stay alive and become a fragment of our illusion of imagination.

Timothy Michael Earwood

This Kiss

When we say goodbye
It tears me up inside
With promises of love with tears
But still the pain resides
When we say goodbye
I hold your hand so tight
With memories of this kiss
I know I'll be all right.

Sounds like the weak crying out

We've become lost in ourselves.

Recycling is one step forward, whereas,

Population is two steps back.

Confused as we are, we hire the mediocre to do the paramount but,

We label the genius insane.

If Christ exists, and if he decides to come back,

His first words will not be, "my children, let's go home,"

But instead, "my children, what have you done?"

We ask, "what can I have" instead of "how can I help?"

Timothy Michael Earwood

Trarattar

Love Lamps, and house clamps
For sale in every home.
Death Swings, porch caskets
A solitary poem.
Grave Teachers and school robbers
A gypsy in the night.
Jazz Dancers and ballet musicians
Walk into the light.

Great Expansion

As I ponder the great expansion called life, I can't help from wondering if it's all in vain.

I mean, what is it all really for?

What is the use to be born, educated, work, have children, and then die, only to pass the gift (or curse) on to your children or many children?

Cursing. Chastising. Pain. Death. Are these the real passions? The only True passions?

We are so apt at mourning and depression. Sometimes, it seems that we welcome it.

Happiness? Joy? Nirvana? Where can these be found when we feel that tomorrow is not worth living?

In Therapy 1

"The raving maniacs made me write poetry, then called me mad."

Who are they?

"They are the raving lunatics."

Are they lunatics?

"Yes; they just don't realize it."

Understand the temptation of everyday life.
Understand the passion for sex.
Understand death.
Understand the understanding that all
understanding is only understanding.

If you wake in a dream, do you feel like you're still in a dream?
"Sometimes when I can't sleep, I lie awake in bed with the lights on, looking up at the ceiling, and then I realize, I'm dreaming."

Crazy like the Wind

Crazy like the wind
so fast, so cold
Driving long all night;
speed on death's highway

Why would you play with my senses,
when you know that I'll die without them?
The path can be open, but
if you're going the wrong way, it creates labor

Gravely

Turning through pages, you'll never understand what it feels
like to die.
I want, but never need.
Don't lie to yourself about necessities when what you really
want…
Ta da!
You want, but never need.
Anything you need is what you really want.
Don't fool yourself or your SELF.

Out of Work

Death so sweet in disguise
The honored truss of my demise
with fooling colors of trick or treat
unfathomed silence 'twas no feat

One

One life, one world,
one heart, one chance.
Not one shoe, or one leg,
but one soul, or one vision.
One fear, one joy,
one essence, one sin.
One notion, one minute,
one death, one void.

Deluded by Simplicity

Buy a gift at a boutique,
Throw in some hash
And think…
Or if you prefer
You go see the apothecary
With dreams of yours
Selling them at a cheap price
For your borrow
Come back tomorrow.
The bodegas around the corner
With the heavenly name
And their bright ideas
And over-priced consumption
Of souls with lost emotions
What would you rather do?

Sonnet #1

O heaven up above the sky so high,
And core of earth below my feet so low;
So many becauses, only one why,
Many versions of yes, one steadfast no.
Lick the stamp, there is no denying time,
But wait enjoy our lives are all-sublime.

3D

Suffrage in disguise
Landscapes of hues
Words whistling in the wind
Wander magnitudes of imagination
Flower power towers for hours
To relight the dim flame of revolution
Say goodnight to your dreams
Nothing's what it seems.

Anonymous

"Oh sheeeit!" the Negro cried out.

Nothing more, nothing less. He died knowing not that his labors were not in vain. That his surpris-ed life fit into the puzzle: the perfect fit.

"One day, I'll be a Negro," the man smiled as he walked away.

The Seasons Change

Dry eyes see roses of uncoupled daisies,

still lie are the ground swallows,

that beg tenderly at the suckling death of deceit.

We die waiting and are born unexpectedly wanting more.

Smile. Smile and be blissfully ignorant;

A cliché; a bastard of insolence.

Cry freedom when love's luster's done fallen like leaves.

Timothy Michael Earwood

Poor Freedom

Jingling change, you make me smile.
What will we buy today?
A bit 'o freedom for a while,
A disparate dream away of bile;
What will they make us pay?
Unpaid bills, bring uncried woes,
Stretch out the bounds of lie.
Without those hounding foes,
In jest without the lows;
Happiness would surely die.

Fishing

Sunshine water
My great father
Casting, reeling
Far, no ceiling
No place to be
We are so free
Let's do again
What made us friends

Blue Bird

Blue bird, why do you fly so high?

Or low, for that fact, I wonder why.

I'm down and you are low,

And when I'm high you seem to know.

Blue bird, don't mistake freedom with free will, or throw caution to the wind.

I made that mistake for you; I saved you a heartache to mend.

Night

The night is evidence that good will still exists.

The night holds dear dreams of honey dew mist.

The night shares with everyone sweet memories.

The lake, the back porch, our last sanity.

The night now seems evil lurking in itself.

The night dejects wishes, provides cover & stealth.

The night holds my secret of riches and wealth.

Puts grown men out to pasture with their spring on a shelf.

Timothy Michael Earwood

Whores of the World

I am the writer
You can suck my cock
So you can say
That you sucked my cock
Why? I don't know
You tell me how cocksucking
Can become a status symbol.

In Space

The death crazed maniac feeds on lost souls;
The star gazing strangers dwell on black holes.
Hopes are so taken; dreams fall awaken,
and little mirrors of truth shine glimpses forsaken.

In the Mouth of Madness

Madness comes in like the wind through a door on a cold winter's night.

Madness comes and goes like savages throughout history that records the lust for time.

But love is there like the hearth that's not required, but warms us at night.

And love is the passion we feel, but cannot explain through any reason or rhyme.

Love's Safe

I love you in Sight

I love you in Home.

I love for all Seasons.

I love you Alone

I love you to Death

I love you Forever

I love for all Reasons

I love you for Never

Never a reason, rhyme, list of time, nor anyone
can 'splain;

Our love is deeper, wider, more intense than any
other can attain.

Diety

sky is translucent
  destiny makes its way
across universes & galaxies
across the Milky Way
instruments of paradise
  we gaze into the sky
wondering
  waiting to believe
   ask why
  in a blink of an eye
filled with doubt,
  we search
for paradise
We never give up hope.
We'll grasp at a fairietale that's dangling from a rope
of an innocent lie that was started long time ago.
Something like a movie, a cinematic show.
One day, sweet child, you'll never know.
Because when dust becomes dust once again there'll be no more tears
there'll be no crying you'll only want to wish to want to have that one chance to make it right

Kerouac's Hope

This day's illusion falls fast, as day turns to night, then night to nothingness.

Then, with a sharp awakening, you are trampled by pale reasoning once again.

Graciously yielding, and tiredly yearning, while your hopes and dreams dangle from a thread of permanence, with wide eyes you seek for treasure chests while the prize rests at the bottom of a dump.

And finding bliss becomes difficult while looking through your tainted lenses.

Close your eyes and feel your way through reality, lest dignanty becomes foolishness, and you fail more miserably than me.

Through insane eyes you find sanity.

Through sane eyes you become more and more insane.

Timothy Michael Earwood

Ode to Wife

I want to feel like I belong
No time to turn away from life
No time to learn and take a wife
Society weeps while celebrities smile
Wish all a happy life
Wish myself a happy wife
Decadence lies and honest anger
Instead, celebrate the gift of life
Instead, celebrate, fellows, your beatific wife

Up, Up, Up

up, up, up
down, down, down
zig, zag, jump, fall
in and out and all around
a, b, c
1, 2, 3
who, what, when, et al
of what kind follows flee or free

Parting the Sea

At different times, we went our separate ways.

Boy meets girl and world meets girl.

Why couldn't you see that life was not a pearl in an oyster found for you and only you?

But, as poems are written in the mind to poets exhibiting their masturbating skills, you can look into the burning eyes,

Eyes that pierce through steel,

Eyes that tell about the old ways,

Eyes that want more understanding,

Eyes that always gaze;

And know what's desired.

Not returned youth, nor riches, nor fame,

Nor lusting fox queens that bring more shame,

But a quiet moment that opens the mind

    & reassures the soul

        & appraises my worth

           & tempts my pride.

Yet, as we go our separate ways,

we're blinded by society's rules, ideas, whims, and queer of all its days.

The Beat, the New Beat

Daisies & Dandelions
    Fresh in the spring
        Which are yellow? Which are white?
Blossomed goddesses
    Smile as they sing
        Playing violins, cellos,
           A quartay actually
Stop! The music stops.
    The beat
It changes
    But the song remains the same
Faithfully sticking to the guns of the game
Violently stroking posers
    Wait in the shadows
        For a glimse of a king
    Their unborn royal intuition
    Looking for the real thing
Dogs lie more happily than some
Who torture themselves in spite of folly
Close your eyes, ears, senses
And experience the rhythm of your
Beat-ta-beat-beat.

Live for life to live

Searching desperately for an answer, we will delude ourselves in the sake of sanity and in the form of reason.

What we are, and more frightening, what we can be, scares us to no end. And fear only wrecks our ability to act within the realm of infiniteness; the beautiful beatitude of a universe of the noumenal conscience that we all possess. It poses as a voice to lead us where we should and should not go. It's not the bright light that you should be worried about, but the vast darkness, the plague of all plagues dancing upon our innocent souls like goblins dancing to a mad violinist's tune of envy and reproach.

Nigh.

Listen.

Be still.

Death settles O so gently.

And wipes away your tears.

Your pains.

Your sorrows.

Every iota of forsaken possibilities. BUT WAIT! It does not come quietly and unannounced. It creeps silently in sound, but with the wisdom that interprets loudly, the message that smacks you in the face. But first, time passes, and so does your past. Your sweet, memorable past. In an instant, it might as well be, so quickly you are at your goal in life, when it was supposed to be so long.

"Please," you ask silently, as you hear your heart slow. Then it speeds, and the air picks you up and rushes through like you're not there.

Comfortable silence.

Music.

Death? Death!

Ignorance, but not bliss. Fright. Anxiety. Pure emotion. Is that what we are? Are we pure emotion trying to attain the impossible? Rationalize our desires.

It's one in the morning, That Lusts Life

This old pen who's soul has seen

> The inside and outside, day & night

And in past life served a different purpose

But only is, because is is.

How can something be so beautiful

> And be so meaningless, without saying?

PSCHK! Becomes meaningful to many.

Girl feels fine

> Boy feels horny

>> Girl ignores boy

>>> Boy lusts for girl

And there are 8 million varieticals to the end of this story.

The scream torments blind souls, but become recognized as laughter within pleasure of unknowledgeable misunderstanding.

Wear your soul on your sleeve, but keep your mind in check and your cunt in mind, but never believe that an address is singular in nature and plurally academic.

Open Eyes

The toothpick airplane flies through the sky,

    Praying tonight that it flies high,

        And no one will die.

A babe waits for me at home,

    Don't want to leave her at home,

        Can you hear the moan?

Clouds reflect in the sea

As the elderly sleeps quietly

The harmony of life and death

Sitting in first class, arguing over souls undisturbed as maniacs fight over raises, pork bellies, and the color of their brand new sedan.

Open eyes can never be taken away,

    Open eyes see brighter days,

        Open eyes, a day in may.

Age of Aquarius

The beautiful meadows set the mood
As most scenetics do
The meadows were beautiful because
Everything else was
      The people
          The music
      The love
      The tears
      The memories
The Age of Aquarius that holds dear,
soft and distant visions of beauty, the original.

Royal Babies

When the winds of war rage
Nothing can contain the fire
    That's fed by the fuel of greed
But don't you know that love
    Conquers all and life
    Lusts for love as war
    Does money
Shame away the consciousness of
    Doubt
And wake the concept of mysticism
    So we can once again
    Understand and walk proudly
    And never again be caught
    Between a rock and
    Society's vegetable laws
    And blind protocols
Mr. God, where ever you are, remove
Our tainted lenses that shield
    The reality and prove your jealousy
    Of us, the kings of the world,
    And rulers of the universe.

Timothy Michael Earwood

Running and Hiding from Myself

Destiny chases me, it binds me to a dream
My futures planned to the point I want to scream
Cry; cry children into the night
We can't see you; please walk into the light.

Your ideas interest me no more
I don't need your values; don't need your foreign wars.
I need freedom from labels and peace of mind of mine
Why does the aura that surrounds the earth always seem sublime?

Love, hate, life, death
The chill of fate steals my breath
Lying still; grating pain
Teach us all marring shame.

Time

The sun set on the misty plain
Where did it go wrong?
Comparable? Wrong. Never; not the same song.
This time it's not…please don't waste my time.
Never mind. Just never mind.
Comparable? Right. It's the same song.

Reality, it's what inside?
People read. Always the wrong side.
Depression sinks in; they say your suicidal.
But you just need time. Transgression. You just need time.

It's trivial. Why? Takes your mind away
Needless things are not the things you find.
It's trivial. High. Blows your mind away.
Fly away.
Flys away.
Needless things. Lie! Say th-th-that you don't mind.

Reality, it's what inside?
People speak. Is humanity wrong?
Depression sinks in. They say it's psychological.
But you just want time. Agression. Direction. You just need time.

Timothy Michael Earwood

Tribute to the Unknown Soldier

Deftly dealing morning's dew
    Amount the sweet spring plans
        Among picnics over rooftops
            Of the images of war
Of was once long ago
    A hero's dream, a beggar's wish
        To have a meal on the table
            A politician's plan to even the score
In armed chairs & executive suites
    Dressed in shiny buttons
        That sees no blood
With a guarantee of piece of mind
    And a pea coat that's clear of mud
So today we celebrate
    And pay a tribute
        With music, food, and ale
For the time long ago
    Whence the blind
        And innocent fell
So we will always remember
    Who, what, when, where
And so that never, ever
    Will we ever again
        Rush in with our care

smells like halloween

his name was not spoken
no one ever saw his face
or the place where he lived
but everyone knew the story
the monster in the forest
the house on the hill
he's ferocious, it's haunted
& the only thing he lives for is to kill
the white werewolf, vampires
what's a goblin anyway?
something that eats you
yellow teeth and matted hair
cause fright on sight
we'll hide under our force field
& wait for unconsciousness
& daylight intrudes
gratefully, thankfully
the sun promises us safety
until the servant of that beast
swallows it, too
and the only thing that can protect us
is ignorance or knowledge
because nothing is true

The Realm Between Here and Now

When the winds of war rage
nothing can contain the fire
       that's fed by the fuel of greed

But don't you know that love
     conquers all and life
         lusts for love as war
           does money

Shame away the consciousness of doubt

And wake the concept of mysticism
     so we can once again
         understand and walk proudly
           and never again be caught
              between a rock and
                 society's vegetable laws
                   and blind protocol

Mr. God, whereever you are, remove our tainted lenses

that shield the reality,

and prove your jealousy of us,

the Kings of The World, and Rulers of the Universe.

Printed in the United States
3394

9 780595 195015